Honeybee
(Endowed nature)

Somefun Muritala

TABLE OF CONTENTS

Pest and disease management

Chapter Ten

Colony Collapse Disorder

Conclusion

Reference

Introduction

The raising, handling, and care of beehives is known as beekeeping. Bees are kept for their honey and other products, or for fun as pollinators of fruit and vegetable blossoms. The practice is common; bees are kept in big cities and villages, on farms and rangelands, in forests and deserts, from the Arctic and Antarctic to the Equator. They are not domesticated; bees living in a man-made home known as a beehive or hive are no different from those living in a colony in a tree.

Back in antiquity, people were aware that bees swarmed to multiply, produced delicious honey, and stung. By the 17th century, they had discovered how effective smoke was in keeping them under control and had created the screen veil to ward off stings. The major discoveries that form the basis of contemporary beekeeping were made between the 17th and the 19th centuries. Among these were the enigma surrounding the queen bee, who is the progenitor of almost every member of the colony, her peculiar method of reproduction, parthenogenetic development, mobile frame hives, and the fact that bees will produce a new queen in the event that the old one vanishes.

With this information, individuals might split a colony rather than depending on spontaneous swarming. Subsequently, the invention of the wax-comb foundation—a starter comb that bees use to construct straight, manageable combs—as well as the realization that honey could be harvested and the combs could be recycled—paved the way for industrial beekeeping and large-scale honey production. The effectiveness of bee colonies in producing honey has grown due to the detection of diseases and the use of medication to treat them, the importance of pollen and pollen replacements in building robust colonies, and the artificial insemination of queens.

Chapter One

The colonies of honeybees

A colony of honeybees is an extremely complex group of individuals that functions almost as a single organism. It typically consists of the queen bee, a fertilized female capable of laying a thousand or more eggs per day; from a few to 60,000 sexually immature females, the worker bees; and from none to 1,000 male bees, or drones. The female of most bee species is venomous. Honeybees are social insects that are well-known for the copious amounts of honey they provide for their nests.

A flower's nectar is being consumed by a honeybee (Apis).
Nectar, a sugary fluid, is harvested by honeybees from nectaries found in flowers and occasionally on plant leaves or stems. After being processed by bees into honey, nectar with a water content of 50–80% will

only contain 16–18% water. On occasion, they gather honeydew, a substance produced by specific insects that feed on plants, and preserve it as honey. Honey is bees' main source of carbohydrates. Additionally, they gather pollen, a dust-like male component found in flower anthers.

The vital proteins required for raising young bees are found in pollen. The bees pollinate the flowers they visit while gathering nectar and pollen to supply the hive. Propolis is a resinous substance that bees gather from tree buds to seal hive breaches and hide foreign objects that they are unable to remove. They gather water to cool the hive and dilute the honey for their own consumption. In a single year, a thriving colony in a prime position might gather and transport up to 1,000 pounds (450

kilograms) of nectar, water, and pollen into
the hive.

Bees excrete beeswax on the underside of
their abdomen, where it solidifies into thin-
walled, six-sided cells resembling
honeycombs. The needs of the colony
determine how the cell is used. Some cells
may be used to store honey or pollen, while
other cells are used by the queen to lay
eggs, usually one egg per cell. The
broodnest is the place where bees hatch
from their eggs. Pollen is typically found in
cells around the broodnest beneath the
honey, and honey is typically stored near
the top of the combs.

Regardless of the outside temperature, the
bees in the broodnest maintain a consistent
temperature of approximately 93 °F (34 °C).
If water is available, the colony can

withstand daily maximum temperatures of 120 °F (49 °C) by using it to air-condition the cluster. The bees stop flying when the temperature drops below roughly 57 °F (14 °C), gather together to store heat, and wait for the weather to warm up again. They can withstand temperatures as low as -50 °F (-46 °C) for several weeks.

Bees lay more eggs, the cluster grows, and honey builds up in the combs when summer flowers blossom profusely. A crowded home results from the enormous number of young bees emerging.

a). Swarming

The worker bees choose a dozen or so tiny larvae that would otherwise become worker bees when the colony fills up with adult bees and there aren't enough cells for the queen to lay many eggs in. Royal jelly, a pale food with a viscosity similar to mayonnaise, is provided in large quantities to these larvae. It is generated by specific brood-food glands located in the worker bees' heads. The larva's growing cell is pulled out and extended to allow for the queen's development. The mother queen leaves the beehive with the swarm not long before these virgin queens emerge as adults from their queen cells.

Swarming typically happens in the midst of a warm day when the queen and a few thousand to twenty-five thousand worker bees abruptly emerge from the hive and take to the air. The queen lands after a few minutes of flying, ideally on a tree branch but occasionally on a roof, a parked car, or even a fire hydrant. Around her, all the bees form a close group, and a few scouts visit a potential new homesite.

The cluster splits once the scout bees have found a new home. The swarm takes to the air, moving toward the new residence in a swirling mass. The bees' natural means of reproduction or growth is swarming.

b). The queen bee

Once the mother queen leaves the parent colony, the first queen to emerge tries to wipe out the others right away. When two or more appear at once, they engage in combat till the last breath. The virgin that survives sets out on her mating flight when she is around one week old. A queen may often mate while in the air (a process known as polyandry) with multiple drones in order to preserve genetic variety within the colony. She may carry out the mating flights two or three times in a row before starting to lay eggs.

She seldom ever again leaves the hive without a swarm. Her sperm pouch, or spermatheca, often contains enough sperm to fertilize every egg she will lay for the remainder of her life. While mating, the drones perish.
Though many beekeepers replace the queen every year or two, the queen can survive up to five years. In the event of her unintentional death or if her egg-laying productivity starts to decline, the worker bees will raise a "supersedure" queen who will mate and deposit eggs without a swarm appearing. The mother queen, who promptly leaves the colony, is disregarded by her.

c). Worker bees

In the active season, worker bees have a six-week lifespan; however, if they emerge as adults in the fall and hibernate in the cluster, they can live for several months. Except from laying eggs, worker bees perform all hive tasks, as their name suggests.

d). Drones

Only in colonies with a large population and an abundance of nectar and pollen sources are drones raised. They typically only survive a few weeks, but when autumn or a protracted time of hardship strikes the colony, they are forced to leave the hive and perish. The drone's sole responsibility is to mate with the queen.
In the drone cells, the queen may lay drone eggs, which are not fertilized. When her

sperm supply runs out or she is forbidden from mating, she will deposit unfertilized eggs in worker cells. Parthenogenesis is the term used to describe the development of unfertilized eggs into adult drones.

A colony may occasionally lose its queen and not be able to produce a new one. Subsequently, a portion of the worker bees start to lay eggs, frequently multiple eggs per cell, which hatch into drones. Requeening a colony with a laying queen might be challenging if laying workers have grown within it.

Chapter Two

Colony modification

A beekeeper gathering a swarm of bees. Early autumn is beekeepers' busiest time of year. At that point, he requeens the colonies whose queens aren't laying enough eggs and ensures that every colony has enough stores—at least fifty pounds, or twenty-two kilograms, of honey, and multiple frames full of pollen. In order to lessen the possibility of nosema disease causing harm to adult bees, some beekeepers also give fumagillin (see below Disease and pest control). The colonies require exposure to sunlight and shielding from chilly winds. In the winter, some beekeepers in mountainous and northern regions wrap their colonies with insulating material. A few beekeepers harvest their honey, kill their bees in the fall, store the empty equipment, and refill the next spring with a two- or three-pound (0.8- or 1.4-kg) package of bees and a young queen.

The colonies don't require much care in the winter if they are prepared correctly in the fall. However, it is crucial for the beekeeper to inspect the colonies in the early spring. Strong colonies often run out of food and starve just a few days before the abundant display of flowers.

Such a starved colony might be saved by little more than a few pounds of sugar syrup, 50/50 sugar water, or a honey-filled comb from another more flourishing colony. The colony may once more be fed fumagillin, and some beekeepers further feed a cake of pollen supplement or alternative. The beekeeper feeds no honey to the colonies unless he is certain of its origins. His hives could become infected with honey from colonies afflicted by American foulbrood, which would result in a significant loss.
The cluster size grows as spring approaches, going from a low population of 10,000 to 20,000 bees that made it through the winter.

The keeper inserts extra supers, or boxes of combs, to accommodate the cluster and broodnest's increased size. The colony is unlikely to swarm if the combs are managed in such a way that the queen can continuously extend her area for depositing eggs upward. Combs that are empty or in which brood is about ready to emerge should be placed near the top of the cluster, while combs that are full with eggs or young brood should be placed toward the bottom of the broodnest. At the start of the main nectar flow, the beekeeper wants the colony to attain its peak number of 50,000–60,000 bees.

After leaving the hive with a belly full of honey, swarming bees seldom ever sting. Typically, to catch them, you have to set up a hive or upside-down box underneath or close by, and then shake or smoke the bees to drive the queen and most of the colony inside. The others have their turn. The swarm can be relocated to a permanent location once it has been placed safely within the box.

Beekeeping regulations typically mandate that the hives housing the bees have moveable combs. Within a few days of being collected in a box, the bees are usually moved into a movable-frame hive to ensure that the fresh honey and comb are not wasted during the movement.

Requeening a colony involves taking out the unsatisfactory or failing queen and replacing her with a new one in the broodnest, which is enclosed in a screen cage. She can be taken out of the cage after a few days when the colony grows accustomed to her. If an unfamiliar queen is placed in the cluster without this temporary protection, the workers will usually murder her right away. Typically, queens are sent in separate cages measuring roughly three cubic inches (50 cubic centimeters), together with roughly six attendant bees and a lump of sugar candy that has been carefully prepared to plug one end of the cage. The candy is consumed by the bees on both sides of the cage when it is placed inside the hive.

When the candy is gone and the bees are close enough to each other to mix up their scents, the queen leaves the cage, enters the colony, and starts laying eggs.

Chapter Three

Equipment for beekeeping

This include a veil to shield the face, gloves for inexperienced beekeepers or those allergic to stings, and a smoker to subdue bees.
Three tools are involved
i). an extractor to remove honey from cells,

ii).an uncapping knife to open honey cells,

iii). and a rough steel blade known as a "hive tool" for separating frames and other hive elements for inspection.

Chapter Four

Bee stings

The barbed sting of a worker bee is ripped off the bee during the stinging process. It contains a poison sac loaded with venom and muscles linked to it that work for many minutes to drive the sting deeper into the skin while also injecting more venom. Instead of grasping and pulling out the sting, it is best to scrape it loose right away to avoid this. Nobody ever develops immune to the agony of bee stings. However, after a few stings, immunity to the swelling normally develops.
The typical response to a bee stung is severe, instantaneous pain at the sting site.

After a minute or two, there is a reddening that may spread up to an inch in diameter. You might not notice swelling until the next day. Acute allergic reactions can occasionally result from a sting; these cases are typically experienced by those with other allergies. Less than an hour later, this type of reaction shows symptoms such severe dyspnea, shock, erratic heartbeat, splotchy complexion, and trouble speaking. Those who fall into this category ought to see a physician right away.

Chapter Five

Bee related products

Liquid, comb, and creamed honey are the many types of honey that are sold. There are instances where the honey's primary flower type is mentioned.

a). Liquid Honey

You can put more supers right above the brood nest if you want liquid (strained, extracted) honey. One gets lifted and another is put underneath once it is almost full. This can go on until the nectar flow stops or until multiple have been filled, each containing between 30 and 50 pounds (14 and 23 kg). With the combs removed, the cells uncapped with the uncapping knife, and the honey extracted, the bees drain the water until the honey reaches the proper consistency and is sealed in the cells. In order to thin it and eliminate yeasts that could lead to fermentation, the extracted honey is instantly heated to roughly 140 °F (60 °C). After being cleared of wax and pollen grains, it is quickly chilled and packed for sale.

b). Comb Honey

To produce honey in the comb, or comb honey, great caution must be taken to keep the bees from swarming. The bees must be packed into the smallest area they can withstand without swarming, and the colony must be robust. Immediately above the brood nest are new frames or pieces of a frame coated with extra-thin foundation wax, supplied at precisely the proper moment to allow the bees to fill without damaging them. The new comb will be of poor quality if the bees do not fill and seal it in time to allow removal in a few days. Up until the nectar flow slows down, new sections are added at the same rate as sections are eliminated. The colony is then given combs to store its honey for the winter after these are removed.

c). Creamed honey

Most honey crystallizes or transforms into sugar. Put the container in water heated to approximately 150 °F (66 °C) to liquefy such honey without significantly compromising its quality. One way to get uniformly fine granulation in liquid and granulated honey is to combine, homogenize, and store at a cool temperature. The honey has a smooth, creamy appearance and is called "creamed honey" if it is processed properly, with fine granules.

d). Flora types

Certain honeys are marketed according to their floral kind, which is the name of the main flowers the bees visited to gather honey. Although the beekeeper cannot guide the bees to a specific food source, he or she can identify the main honey-producing plants via expertise. The hues and flavors of honey produced by various flowers vary. It can have a dark or light body type, a strong or mild flavor, and a heavy or thin body type. The majority of honey has been combined by beekeepers to a uniform quality that may be sold and provided annually.

Chapter Six

Pollination

Bees are most valuable when they are used
as pollinators. Approximately ninety crops
grown in the United States alone rely on
insect pollination, which is mostly carried

out by honeybees. When it comes to crop pollination, the average bee colony is worth 20–40 times as much as when it comes to honey production. It has never been determined how important bees are to the pollination of decorative plants. Additionally, bees play a crucial role in the pollination of some forest and range plants that yield seeds that serve as food for birds and other species.

When a beekeeper uses bees to pollinate crops, the colonies are placed within or close to the crop that needs to be pollinated. Most of the approximately one million colonies utilized for pollination are found in apple and almond orchards, as well as in fields of alfalfa seed. In alfalfa fields, the colonies are spaced out in groups of 0.1 mile (0.16 km) apart, with two or more colonies per acre. For almond orchards, two colonies per acre are advised, and for apple orchards, around one colony per acre. While some farmers want the colonies spread out in tiny clusters within the orchard, others would rather have them put alongside the orchard. Bees are also routinely utilized by producers of numerous other crops: plums, cutflower seed, cucumbers, cranberries, cherries, clovers, blueberries, and cantaloupes

Chapter Seven

The Colony and Its Structure

Because honey bees are social insects,
they reside in sizable, cohesive family
groups. Highly evolved social insects
perform a wide range of intricate tasks that
the vast majority of solitary insects do not
execute. To survive in social colonies,
honey bees have evolved a variety of skills,
including division of labor, communication,

sophisticated nest building, defense, and environmental control. Because of these amazing habits, social insects in general—and honey bees in particular—are some of the most fascinating animals on the planet.

Three types of adult bees are usually found in a honey bee colony: workers, drones, and a queen. Thousands of worker bees collaborate to construct nests, gather food, and care for their young. Every member has a certain duty pertaining to their mature age to fulfill. But the colony as a whole must work together to survive and procreate. Workers, drones, and queens are the individual bees that depend on the colony for survival.
During late spring and summer, a colony typically consists of several hundred drones and a single queen in addition to thousands of worker adult. The queen and workers'

presence preserves the colony's social structure, which also depends on an efficient communication system.

The actions required for colony life are managed by communicative "dances" and the delivery of chemical pheromones among members. Worker bees' labor activities are mostly determined by their age, though they can also change depending on the demands of the colony. The size of the worker force, the number of food storage, and the queen all affect reproduction and colony strength. Both the colony's size and efficiency grow until they reach a maximum of roughly 60,000 workers.

Except for the period immediately before and after swarming preparations or supersedure, each colony has a single queen. She serves as the sole sexually mature female, hence reproduction is her main duty. She yields eggs that are both fertilized and unfertilized. The spring and early summer are when queens lay the most eggs. A queen's daily egg output might reach 1,500 during its peak. Early October marks the gradual end of their egg-laying, and they don't lay many or any until early January of the following year. A single queen has the capacity to lay up to 250,000 eggs annually and maybe over a million over her lifetime.

It is easy to identify a queen from other colony members. Typically, her body is far longer than that of the worker or drone, particularly during the egg-laying phase when her abdomen enlarges significantly. While the wings of workers and drones almost reach the tip of the abdomen when folded, her wings only cover about two-thirds of the belly. A queen lacks functional wax glands and pollen baskets, and her thorax is slightly larger than a worker's. Compared to the worker, her stinger is longer and more curved, but it also has fewer, shorter barbs. Although the typical productive life span of a queen is two to three years, she can live up to five years.

The production of pheromones, which act as a social "glue" to bring a bee colony together and aid in fostering individual identity, is a queen's secondary role. Her mandibular glands create one main pheromone, known as queen substance, but there are other significant ones as well. The queen's ability to lay eggs and produce chemicals determines the colony's characteristics in great part. The genetic composition of the drones she has mated with and herself greatly influences the colony's size, disposition, and quality.

After emerging from a queen cell, the queen stays out of the hive for about a week, spending that time mating with multiple drones in flight. In order to avoid inbreeding, she must fly a considerable distance from her colony to mate, thus she first circles the hive to get her bearings. She disappears for almost thirteen minutes after leaving the hive by herself. Usually in the afternoon, the queen mates with seven to fifteen drones at a height of more than twenty feet. The queen has a chemical odor that drones can detect and identify (pheromone). The queen loses her capacity to mate and can only lay unfertilized eggs, which develop into drones, if inclement weather prevents her from flying for more than 20 days during her mating flight.

Within 48 hours of mating, the queen returns to the hive and starts producing eggs. Every time she lays an egg that will eventually become a worker or a queen, she discharges several sperm from the spermatheca. She does not release sperm if her egg is deposited in a larger drone-sized cell. The worker bees in the colony tend to the queen and feed her royal jelly on a regular basis. The quantity of food the queen is fed and the size of her worker force—which is needed to prepare beeswax cells for her eggs and tend to the larvae that will hatch from the eggs in three days—determine how many eggs she lays. When the amount of substance secreted by the queen runs out, The staff gets ready to surpass (replace) her. After supersedure, the old queen and her new daughter might stay in the hive for a while.

From fertilized eggs or from immature worker larvae that are no older than three days, new (virgin) queens are created. Three conditions are used to raise new queens: swarming, supersedure, and emergency. When an elderly queen is unintentionally killed, misplaced, or extracted, the bees choose younger worker larvae to create backup queens. The worker cells used to create these queens are altered such that they hang vertically on the surface of the comb. The colony gets ready to raise a new queen when an older one starts to fail (lower production of queen material).

Due to the fact that supersedure queens obtain more nourishment (royal jelly) during growth, they are typically superior to emergency queens. Supersedure queen cells are usually raised on the comb surface, just like emergency queen cells. On the other hand, queen cells that are ready to swarm are located in the spaces between the beeswax combs in the brood region or at the bottom edges of the frames.

a). Drones

The largest bees in the colony are called drones, or male bees. Usually, they are only around in the late spring and summer. The compound eyes of the drone connect at the top of its head, giving it a much larger head than either the worker or the queen. Drones lack wax glands, pollen baskets, and stingers. Fertilization of the virgin queen during her mating trip is their primary duty. About a week after emerging, drones reach sexual maturity and quickly perish during mating. Drones don't do anything valuable for the hive, yet their existence is thought to

be necessary for the colony to function normally.
Drones typically feed themselves within the hive after four days, although they can also rely on workers for sustenance.

The food supply of the colony may be further stressed by an excessive number of drones because they consume three times as much food as workers do. After they are around eight days old, the drones remain in the hive and start their orientation flights. Typically, the bees take off from the hive between midday and 4:00 p.m. There have never been any reports of drones stealing food from flowers.
Drones are typically driven outside into the cold and left to starve when fall brings cold weather and a shortage of pollen and nectar nutrients. On the other hand,

queenless colonies permit them to remain in the hive indefinitely.

b).Workers

The majority of bees in a colony are workers, who are the smallest. Since they are immature females, they do not deposit eggs in a typical hive. Beekeepers are equipped with unique features, like pollen baskets, smell glands, wax glands, and brood food glands, that enable them to carry out all hive tasks. During their first few weeks as adults, they clean and polish the cells, feed the brood, tend to the queen, clear debris, handle incoming nectar, construct beeswax combs, guard the entrance, and air-condition and ventilate the hive. They later forage for nectar, pollen, water, and propolis (plant sap) as field bees.

In the summer, a worker's lifespan is approximately six weeks. Fall-raised workers can live up to six months, which helps the colony survive the winter and raises new generations before they perish in the spring.

c). Laying workers

The development of several workers' ovaries and the laying of unfertilized eggs occur when a colony loses its queen. It is thought that the brood and the queen's chemicals prevent the workers' ovaries from developing fully. The colony has likely been queenless for one or more weeks if laying workers are present. In normal "queenright" colonies, however, laying workers can also be found during the swarming season and when the colony is led by a bad queen.

There are eggs on the sides of the cell rather than at the base, where a queen deposits them, and laying workers distribute their eggs more haphazardly throughout the brood combs. A considerable number of the drone larvae that do hatch do not make it to maturity in the smaller cells, and some of these eggs never hatch.

Chapter Eight

Bee development

Before becoming adults, all three species of honey bees go through three phases of development: the egg, larva, and pupa. All three phases are referred to as brood. Although the developmental phases are comparable, their durations vary. Fertilized eggs develop into either workers or queens, while unfertilized eggs become drones. The development of female bee castes is influenced by nutrition; larvae intended to become workers receive less royal jelly and more of a mixture of honey and pollen than the queen larva, which receives vast amounts of royal jelly.

a). Egg

The queen of honey bees typically lays one egg per cell. Each egg resembles a little grain of rice and is affixed to the bottom of the cell. The egg stands straight up on end when it is first laid. But the egg starts to bend over during the course of the three-day development phase. The larval stage starts on the third day, when the egg hatches into a tiny grub.

b). Larvae

Pearly white and sparkling, healthy larvae have this appearance. On the bottom of the cell, they are coiled into a "C" form. Larvae capitulate their worker, queen, and drone cells at roughly five and a half, six, and six and a half days, respectively. While still within their beeswax cells, they are fed by adult worker bees, or nursing bees, during the larval stage. The prepupal stage is the time immediately following cell capped. The larva still resembles a grub at this point, but it has lengthened within the cell and spun a thin, silken cocoon. During the prepupal stage, larvae continue to be shiny, plump, and pearly white.

c). Pupae

The prepupae begin to transform from their larval phase into adult bees within the individual cells sealed with a beeswax cover supplied by adult worker bees. During the early stages of development, healthy pupae stay white and shiny despite their bodies starting to resemble adult forms. The first characteristic to change in color is the compound eyes, which go from white to a brownish-purple hue. The remainder of the body soon starts to resemble an adult bee in terms of color. After their cells are capped, new workers, queens, and drones appear 12, 7, ½, and 14 ½ days later, respectively.

Brood patterns

Capped brood makes it simple to identify healthy brood patterns. Healthy capped worker brood frames often feature a consistent pattern with few cells that the queen misses throughout the egg-laying process. Cappings are convex, medium brown in tone, and puncture-free. Drone brood is typically seen in patches at the comb's edges; due to developmental time, the ratio should be four times as many pupae as eggs and twice as many larvae.

Chapter Nine

Pest and disease management

Diseases that damage the brood, diseases that solely affect the adult bees, insect enemies of the adults and of the comb, and other adversaries including toads, lizards, birds, mice, skunks, and bears are all present in honeybee habitats.

a). Disease

The most dangerous brood illness is American foulbrood, which is brought on by the spore-forming bacterium Bacillus larvae. It affects workers, drones, and queens and happens everywhere bees are housed. The spores have a high level of chemical and heat resistance. The mixing of healthy capped brood and diseased or vacant cells that were previously filled by diseased brood gives a comb harboring highly infected brood a mottled look. Digging into the rotting bulk reveals a peculiar ropiness that makes it easily identifiable.

Bees can contract American foulbrood by eating honey from contaminated colonies or by moving equipment to healthy colonies. To manage the illness, terramycin and sulfathiazole are frequently utilized. Bee inspectors are tasked with enforcing legislation for the elimination of unhealthy colonies by fire in numerous nations, including most states in the United States. Bacillus alvie and Acromobacter eurydice are frequently linked to Streptococcus pluton, the nonsporeforming bacterium that causes European foulbrood. The look of this illness resembles that of American foulbrood.

In certain cases, it damages the colonies significantly, but they bounce back, negating the need to destroy them. The illness can be managed with terramycin. On the surface, sacbrood and foulbrood diseases are similar, and both are caused by viruses. Though it rarely gets serious, it might unexpectedly emerge and disappear. Chemical control is not required. The beekeeper typically requeens the colony if the issue continues.

Ascosphaera apis is the fungus that causes chalk brood. The disease's larval victims have a powdery white look. Aspergillus flavus is a fungus that causes stonebrood in bees, and it can typically be isolated from the affected bees. Stonebrood affects both adults and brood.

The most dangerous condition affecting adult bees is Nosema illness, which is brought on by the microsporidian Nosema apis. It is very common, severely weakens colonies, and results in significant losses in honey output. When bees have nosema disease, the symptoms are not visible from the outside. Adults contract the disease from one another by consuming the spores, which quickly germinate in the major stomach, known as the ventriculus. A soft, bloated, grayish white ventriculus is typically the result of infection. Fumigillin is a medication that can be fed to the colony to achieve some control.

The mite Acarapis woodi, which enters the bee's tracheae by its spiracles or breathing pores in its thorax or abdomen, is the cause of acarine illness. This mite causes dislocated wings, enlarged abdomens, and flightlessness in bees. For now, there is no effective control for this mite. The sole federal legislation governing bees in the United States was created to stop adult bees containing this mite from being imported into the country.

Beekeepers face significant challenges from two other mite species that are native to Asia: Tropilaelaps clareae and Varroa destructor. Nowadays, V. destructor is frequently seen in North America and Europe, where it can wipe out whole bee colonies.

Adult bees can also suffer from other minor ailments, but they rarely result in significant issues.

b). Pest

In its larval state, the larger wax moth, or Galleria mellonella, is a lepidopterous insect that demolishes combs. Although it doesn't kill mature bees, it can start destroying a poor colony's combs long before the bees themselves disappear. It can also ruin honey combs that have been preserved. When the larvae are ready to pupate, they frequently destroy frames and other hive components by eating away at the soft wood of the hive where they would normally spin their cocoons. Maintaining robust colonies is the best way to control this problem. Combs that are being stored are either stacked to create a strong air draft around them, fumigated, or housed in a cool room.

Similar to that of the bigger wax moth, stored combs are harmed by the larvae of the lesser wax moth, Achroia grisella. Anagasta kuehniella, the larva of the

Mediterranean flour moth, damages the combs by feeding on pollen. The management approach for these two moths is identical to that of the larger wax moth. Occasionally discovered on bees, Braula caeca, a tiny wingless fly member, is known as the bee louse. It consumes honey or nectar from its host's mouthparts. Its larvae dig burrows in the honeycomb cappings. Sometimes ants break into hives and kill or disturb the bees. Parts of a beehive buried in the ground may be destroyed or damaged by termites.

The honeybee's natural adversaries include other insects including some wasps and yellow jackets (Hymenoptera), praying mantises (Orthoptera), robberflies (Diptera), ambush bugs (Hemiptera), and dragonflies (Odonata).

c). Predators

In winter, when the bees are gathered together, mice often break into the hive or get into stored combs, where they eat through the combs and frames to build their nests. Usually at night, skunks eat a great deal of bees near the entrance to the hive. They are targeted by poison, traps, and fences. Bears typically destroy the hive and all of its contents in order to consume the honeybees and their young. Electric fences and traps are employed to keep bee colonies safe in bear area.
Sometimes bees turn become their own deadly adversaries. When honey is introduced to them in moderate weather and without flowers in bloom, different colonies of bees will compete for it.

Occasionally, this robbing, or warring, gets violent and moves like a mob from hive to hive. Honey is swiftly taken and transported to other hives if all the bees in a colony are dead. This increases the robbery to the point that a cluster that was just minutes before bringing honey into its hive is attacked, all of its occupants are slain, the honey is stolen once more, and the cycle repeats. Usually, the only things that put an end to robbery when it gets serious are darkness and bad weather.

Chapter Ten

Colony Collapse Disorder

Colony collapse disorder, or CCD, is one of
the most enigmatic diseases to affect

honeybee colonies in the contemporary day. It is distinguished by an abrupt demise of the colony and a dearth of adult bees that are healthy inside the hive. The condition seems to impair the adult bees' ability to navigate, while the underlying reason is unknown. After they search for pollen, they never come back to the hive. In the hive, honey and pollen are typically found, along with signs of recent brood raising. There are situations where the queen and a few survivor bees might stay in the brood nest.

Other characteristics of CCD include slower than usual invasion by common pests like wax moths and small hive beetles, as well as delayed stealing of the honey in the dead colonies by nearby, healthy bee colonies. It seems that only the European honeybee (Apis mellifera) is impacted by the condition.

A Pennsylvania commercial beekeeper who had 80–90% colony losses reported CCD for the first time in the fall of 2006. Throughout the spring and summer of 2007, beekeepers in 35 states throughout the US continued to report colony losses; many of them had lost anything from 30 to 90 percent of their hives.

Significant losses of honeybees were also reported by beekeepers in Canada, Portugal, Italy, Spain, Greece, Germany, Poland, France, and Switzerland. The syndrome continued to affect honeybee colonies in the ensuing years, but the annual proportion of colonies lost seemed to be decreasing. However, honeybees have a significant potential economic impact on agriculture; in the United States alone, they pollinate an estimated $15 billion worth of crops annually.

Numerous diseases and parasites, such as viruses, Nosema species, and the phorid fly Apocephalus borealis, have been found in adult honeybee carcasses from impacted colonies.

The presence of pathogens, which can be common in honeybee colonies and pose a constant threat, as well as a compromised immune system brought on by colony stress are some of the factors that many scientists believe are at play, but they have not been able to determine conclusively whether a single pathogen is the primary cause of the disorder. Furthermore, pesticides that are suspected of causing or exacerbating CCD include neonicotinoids, which are insecticides derived from nicotine and hazardous to honeybees.

Conclusion

Beekeeping produces beeswax as a byproduct. Beekeepers attempt to save the beeswax when they break or uncap honeycombs or have unsuitable combs. They start by extracting or draining as much honey as they can from the combs. Once the material is slightly over 145 °F (63 °C), it is placed in water. The wax melts as a result, rising to the top. The wax cake is taken out and polished for use in comb foundation once it has cooled and solidified. In addition to candles, beeswax is used in cosmetics, agriculture, manufacturing, and the arts. Bees are largely controlled in some places to produce wax. Due to its extreme stability, wax may be transported over great distances in unfavorable conditions without experiencing any damage.

In order to create new colonies or replenish weak ones, queens are raised and sold to other beekeepers for use in requeening established colonies or added to packages weighing two or three pounds (0.9 or 1.4 kg). The queens are created when the beekeeper encloses the dominant queen in a colony and introduces between thirty and sixty queen cell bases into the cluster, wherein immature worker larvae (one-day old) have been placed. Although most beekeepers prefer to let the queens mate spontaneously, they can be artificially inseminated with sperm from drones belonging to a known source. Live bees are transferred into cages made of screen wire by shaking them out of the colony's combs using a funnel.

Reference

1).

http://www.canr.udel.edu

2).

http://sciencedirect.com

3).

http://extension.psu.edu

4).

www.nature.com

5).

http://www.aphis.usda.gov